Thoughts From a King

Ryan King

Charleston, SC
www.PalmettoPublishing.com

Thoughts From a King

First Edition

Hardcover ISBN: 979-8-88590-424-7
Paperback ISBN: 978-1-63837-172-4

Biography

Hey young world!!! My name is Ryan King. I am a Human. I am made up of all things that I have come across in this world. I am a teacher. I teach Health, PE, and Sex Education. I am also our school's Athletic Director, and head soccer coach. I have a beautiful wife named Kimberly. Between us we have 3 boys that we share with the world. I am also an advocate for special needs children as I have one of my own named Cooper. As a family we try to raise inspiration to be better people and raise awareness of the beauty of life that others may take for granted. Having the ability to vent and write is how this project started. Some of my writings have helped people in some troubled times, by letting them know they are not alone in feeling certain ways. Hopefully it can do the same for some of the people who come across this book.

I am from Savannah, Georgia. I just moved out of the city to enjoy raising my kids in Richmond Hill, Georgia. It's coastal living at its finest. I love an active lifestyle and to have opportunities to cook and entertain others in my circle of friends and family. Be nice to others, spread love, and be open to new experiences.

Peace!

Table of Contents

Abstract Thoughts

THINK B4 U SPEAKER · · · 1
KEEP BREATHING · · · 2
LIQUID FEELINGS · · · 3
1000 EYES · · · 4
A MAN SAID TO THE UNIVERSE (RESPONSE) · · · 5
RHYTHM OF MY LIFE SONG · · · 6
THE SUNS SHADOW · · · 7
HEARING THE BOTTOM · · · 8
POISON YOUR MIND · · · 9
HOW I FEEL ABOUT "THAT" · · · 10
A TRIP TO THE STORE · · · 11
A DIFFERENT VIEW · · · 12
THE PURPOSE OF LIFE · · · 13
WHERE DOES 1 GO? · · · 14

Thoughts About Myself

DRAVET DAD · · · 15
THE SUICIDE KING · · · 16
AM I A MASTERPEICE IN THE MAKING · · · 17
IN MY HUMAN VAULT · · · 18
4 A MAN WHO CANT COMPLAIN · · · 19
MY LAST THOUGHT · · · 20
A MOTHER'S PATHWAY · · · 21

Thoughts About Family

MOM · · · 22
MY DAD · · · 23
MY LITTLE BOY · · · 24
LOOKING INTO COOPER'S HEART · · · 25
MY GRANDMOTHER'S HAND · · · 26
GRANDPARENTS 50TH WEDDING ANNIVERSARY · · · 27

Thoughts About Love

A BEAUTIFUL GIFT · · · 28
CUPID'S ASSASSIN · · · 29
MY MATCH · · · 30
MY VOW · · · 31
TAKE A WALK WITH ME BABY IN THE GA RED CLAY · · · 32
THOUGHTS OF YOU ON THIS EARTH · · · 34
TO A MAN I'VE NEVER MET. · · · 35
YOU · · · 36

My Thoughts on Haiku's

FRUSTRATED BY QUESTIONS
POPPING THE QUESTION
I HELP STUDENTS
STUDENTS HELP ME · · · 37

ALMOST MY LAST TEXT
VERA
60-YEAR-OLD KISS
IMAGINARY RULES · · · 38

CORN DOG
BIG COOKIE
CHICKEN STEW
UNKNOWN GOOD · · · · · · · · · · 39

Think B4 U Speaker

Having a voice. To use as a guide, weapon, threat, or any other means of force that starts with sound. Simple noises with immediate reactions and tolls on those that are unaware that you are even speaking. One voice or two voices, which is valued more? The argument between two longtime enemies. Or the agreement between the two criminal masterminds. All of the sounds come together to form our history but the truth of some of these renowned conversations that are forever quoted sometimes didn't even happen. Lies. All voices are heard but the way we interpret them is what makes a voice heard. Hearing the right voice can send chills through the toughest of humans. Hearing that one particular voice can make a person want to do the unthinkable. It can make your own voice change. Change tempo, pitch, tone, and even the strength of your message that you are trying to get heard. Everyone has a voice! Not everyone is meant to be heard! The ones that are heard are the people who can make a difference. If you do not speak, nobody can hear, therefore your voice is waiting for its moment. You alone can speak, but if the audience is absent, it is like your voice has never existed!

Rethink and speak louder!

KEEP BREATHING

All I can do is keep breathing. Though in times I hold my breath when things are rough, I know I can stare out the window of the world and focus on the answer being somewhere out there. No matter what happens, I keep breathing. Not even thinking to do so, but necessary to keep going, keep searching, keep hoping that I will be in the state of mind where all my concerns and problems fly away in the breeze that makes me cool on a hot day. As I cool down with the feeling of relief, I remember imagining that small answer through the window of hope. I remember seeing it, yet it seemed so far away! But I'm there now, because I kept breathing. Knowing that if I just kept one foot after the other and took my time, I would reach my pinnacle to where concerns could not reach. Problems could not reach. I am at the top. Still breathing and looking through a bigger window! A window that shows me a different distant object! Unable to identify what it is. I take a big breath. I feel that cool breeze. I lift my foot even though is seems to weigh a million pounds and I begin a new journey. One foot after the other until I reach my last known breath and I'm on the other side of that window!

LIQUID FEELINGS

A single tear can be defined in so many ways. It is usually that feeling when the emotion kicks in the most. The strongest part of your reflected memory. It can hurt, make you happy, grieve, and show your pride or your weakness. A single tear sets the longest path. You notice it gather as your emotions become overwhelming. You balance it like life's biggest decisions. You either let it fall and feel the whole drop of tear run down your cheek, or you fight it so hard until it feels like 10 buckets were poured from your soul but it just produces that one meaningful tear that does not ease down your face. It falls straight to the floor and breaks the levy for the storm of tears that are to follow! This one powerful drop of emotion is always temporary! Liquid feelings!

1000 EYES

I'm not afraid of 1000 eyes! Show my true colors as others may rise. Surprises, they come everlasting in my dreams. Ripped at the seams is my hope that once lived. Pain of my life, is it worth it to give? Life forever, shows, dedication for knowledge we grow. No ideas are of mine worth the effort to spread! Before we turn the page, we all guess the words to be said! Simple and plain. Plain looks very simple.

A Man Said to the Universe

"Sir, I exist!"
"However," replied the universe,
"The fact has not created in me
a sense of obligation."

Response to "A Man Said to the Universe"

"A Journey for Purpose"
What is my purpose, present in time?
Stepping from the shadows, I'm trying to find.
How can I get there? I climb to the top, nobody's waiting.
It's like that a lot. Is anyone out there? Does anyone care?
I look all around, I stop, and I stare.
I see through my eyes, and I know what I've seen.
I visualize my journey on accomplishing my dream.
Time waits for no man, and seconds never stop.
Life is what you make of it; its questions all need thought!

What is a human being's purpose? To be noticed - you must step from the shadows. Choose your path in life, and aim high, even if nobody's around to see your accomplishments you have inner strength to remember times of challenging yourself and the victorious act of accomplishing your life's goals or dreams. Time waits for no one. Seconds can be wasted or developed into dreams beyond your beliefs. You must be in control of your dreams and aspirations. You can do it. It's your life!

RHYTHM OF MY LIFE SONG

Your heart keeps beating to the rhythm of my life song. No matter if you were on one side of the world, I would hear your love. The music in your mind would always find its way to my soul. Little pieces of you flowing in the currents of this world. They search and discover my rhythm even when we are apart. They have found me before I knew you. This song just waiting to be played as we finally meet. It's even more beautiful because I know you hear it too! When everyone stares and sees our presence, it's because your radiance of a beautiful life melody is what they know. No matter if I leave, you will always know the words to our beautiful song! It was destined to be made and the words are engraved on your heart. The rhythm of your life and the harmony of mine. A unique ballad of a story of what is meant to be heard by the world. Our life song! My favorite song! It's played in our hearts.

The Suns Shadow

You must have faith in the sun. It will rise daily and illuminate the darkness. Dark turns into light and shadows are all temporary. Illumination is the brightening of a soul that begs to be seen. It comes as a reflection from the glistening hopes of what one's true intentions are expected to portray. Few people have no faith that days will be brightened and focus on the darker side of the hour. However, the darkness too has its own way of becoming transparent. Just when you the think the maze of darkness is impenetrable, the moon illuminates the way. Just open your eyes and let the guidance of faith find you. Running from a natural guide is how one may choose to give up in the purpose of life. Let the illumination take you and guide you to where your true intentions have planted its intentions for you to be this whole time. Now you are where you are meant to be. No more depending on the bright sunshine, more so the guidance of an illuminated path from a moon's guidance. Now you are your own light and have found the way to be the star you were meant to be in this lifetime. Only now your job is done, and you have left the world of paths and darkness only to light the way for others based on your faith as the bright burning star that you have become from your dedication to stay in the positive light!

Shine bright!

HEARING THE BOTTOM

Having the ability to see the top should not prevent you from still hearing the bottom! Equality of human existence is shattered when it is judged by what you see as a faulted difference. Differences how? Compared to what? Who sets this standard and bar? A complete guess due to the unknown or abnormal through your eyes. A past that you will never understand unless you are willing to listen, much less ask! Yet a person may take an instant to determine character from others. We'll look in the mirror of hypocrisy. You have verbally established what you and most would never want in return. Judgment. Relatable content between human eyes is more so to happen when conversation is indulged and welcome. You close the invitation for empathy and understanding by judging. A more powerful and negative influential brand than most will ever realize. One can only understand the retribution of their actions that they have cast upon others when it's their own kid coming and complaining of the same harshness of words that have been placed on their heart. By then it is too hard to rectify what others have already encountered. It's never too late to apologize. Stop the bullying. Understand peace and love towards humanity. Verbally build up all those around you and try to help rebuild what you have contributed to bringing down.

POISON YOUR MIND

Poison your mind with this rubbish that I speak, let it seep, even thinking deep when I sleep. Into your mind, as my thoughts wear thin, hating the famous and I do not pretend. Make it a goal to hate myself in the end. Never will the blind be able to look. Senses can tell if you mean well or if you're a crook. How tall is the tallest when there's no limit in sight? Wronging your right. Give up on your fight. Answering the questions that are not taken light. Words are made to rewrite. That's the quest, as I invest for this test, and hope that all humans may bless, but they don't, so I guess, now the waters are too strong to test. How do I know the road I'm walking is not a huge guess? Stress! No, as I tend to look away, there is no time for temptation today, straighten my path, not to be guided the wrong way, to clarify, I'm only focused for that strong pay. The objective at hand just to better as man, but just to clarify we got a long way!

HOW I FEEL ABOUT "THAT"

Well, here is how I feel about that, should I hate a person or squash it flat? One could only think of the long-term conditions as once I make this decision; I know that it will affect my whole life. Balance of evil vs good strong in my conscience. Who will win the battle? One thought will. The stronger one. So, what does it come down to? Pride over a simple anger that can be proven as a huge event, or peace deep within begging you not to do this! It grows harder, scratching to the top before the absolute worst happens. My reality is that I'm getting closer to the end. Hoping that my inner strength will prevail, but for my outcry the reality is my voice is raining darkness. All stops around me as I'm singled out with fury. The purity still fighting to be seen. Who will win, my current actions or the good intentions inside begging to be vocally enhanced to its fullest capability? Only one person could tell us. That is me because this is my thoughts! Thanks to you!

A TRIP TO THE STORE

I had a little itch, so I went to the store.
I had 3.75, but cigarettes cost more!
I did not know what to do, so I acted like a bum.
I asked the store clerk if I could only buy one.
If I let you buy one, then you'll ask for two,
Don't you understand? Cigarettes will be the death of you!
I said I did not care, saw a glimmer over there,
I found a shiny quarter, enough to buy the squares.
"Gimme a pack of Kool's, mentholated please"
I put one in my mouth, and my fire met tobacco leaves.
My lungs filled up with smoke, and chemicals galore.
I did this for a year or so, as I was walking from the store.
As I continued smoking, my body started feeling strange.
Don't forget to mention, it's getting harder to find spare change.
I find myself still waiting, in the doctor's office instead.
Cigarettes have taken its toll, and now I cough up red.
I looked up at the doctor, and he looked back at me.
Either you can't quit this habit or next it's RIP.
A man that kept on smoking with 4.00 gripping tight,
How much is in your hand? Will you spend it right?

Dedicate to my high school health class

A DIFFERENT VIEW

Blinded by the present, my future unable to look,
Learning lessons from living, instead of knowledge from a book.
When a hand is offered down, you should grip it tight!
It could be the answer, of understanding fright.
Strong by will, yet weakened by your view,
Looking through your eyes, I see the world anew.
Taking one step at a time, going one foot after the other.
Watch over your friends and know who art thou brother.
Recognize the good, and separate the bad,
Celebrate the wonderful, and do not shame the sad.
If we ever part, and go our separate ways,
I hope these words can help you, to shine on better days.

What I think blind people see.

THE PURPOSE OF LIFE

Tell me the purpose of life and help me escape the pain.
Show me the colors of the wind, and how to feel God's tears
of Rain.
Why must a killer kill? Why must a doctor save? A man's intentions cannot be held back, until
he is in his
Grave.

Mom and Dad, why are you so hard on your son?
Is it to escape the life that once made you run?
Not rich with money, better yet, family and pride.
Hatred and tears are determined as we both feel the same inside.

Show me the purpose of life, a task only time can do.
From a child to a parent, then experience birth as anew.
Now I am a teacher, ands lessons await to be taught.
The purpose of life is earned, something never bought.

WHERE DOES 1 GO?

Where does 1 go, when the last 1 says goodbye?
Trained to think up, down, or maybe through the sky.
She says that "I am here, it's hard to see myself as dead"
My spirit is defined through the knowledge I have spread.
Physically departed, yet my quotes still influence life.
I've helped to understand the meaning of pain as well as strife.
So where does 1 go, as the questions will soon be asked.
You will finally seek your answer if you wait for life to pass.
Scary, calm, and peaceful, all trapped into 1.
Hell, hath no fury, or do I enter Kingdom Come?
Where does 1 go, when they have said their last Goodbyes?
I wondered all this to myself, as I saw her close her eyes.

DRAVET DAD

What a test... being a dad. A father. The key ingredient to raising an honest little boy into a man himself. When odds are stacked against you by God's gift of a child that is anything but regular. This special gift. This special lifelong test that is predicted to not last a lifetime for my little boy. Being single without a partner. However, I have been blessed with two little buddies and believe it or not an amazing one-of-a-kind animal to bring the definition to light of what is now my FAMILY. My own little world. Something that people say I'm great at but when they get a small sample of my reality, they could never fully understand what I go through daily. This is just a look from what is shown from the outside perspective. Having someone you love so much and that reason for breathing not being promised a guaranteed breath tomorrow is the hardest thing I have ever had to experience in life. Yet, I can't let it show. Not in my awaken hours can it show in front of family, friends, coworkers, and even in my own reflection at certain times. I must be strong! Strong for my other son, his brother, his own view of such joy to assure him that he is currently in company with the best possible people that he can be around. I'm jealous. He has so much love that he puts out. Some people say I'm strong. It has no comparison of the amount of strength that I see him endure. Nobody knows. Nobody understands. The truth will never be witnessed. They think I'm ok! A yawn embraces the thought from others that I'm just tired. The reality is because I cherished staying up until 3 am watching him sleep in peace! Breathing softly. Breathing. Being promised breath after breath. Rubbing my hands through his hair. Holding his little hand in comparison of what I hope will grow into the size of mine one day. Shedding tears in silence and dark of the night, allowing myself the only time that I can be weak without a witness. The real reason I'm tired! Worth it. I live every day to the fullest with him. I regret every instance that I was not as patient as I should have been. I am that man because this is my open book test that I must pass! Not for myself. For Cooper. My son. My strength and reason for living without giving up on any situation. The world will never know how hard it is! The thought in the back of my mind lingers like a cancerous cell begging to spread. I hold it back naturally and will fight it until my last breath. Or until his! I love Cooper as much as he loves the World!

-Dravet Dad

The Suicide King

Mighty as he may seem to be. No one can see unless his own eye investigates the reflection. Suspiciousness of his next move. Knowing wrong and knowing right. Really being truthful to oneself. Literally doing what is correct and standing up for it without a mask to disguise the real reason of dishonesty. When the reflection catches up with who is looking at it, the split happens. Good versus bad. Inner versus outer. Top against bottom. Regardless, a dark new path being traveled is hard to navigate blindly for a person who has such a spotlight role. People look for guidance as your navigation controls their moves as well. Such responsibility and even more so, SUCH Pressure!!! But therefore, you have been placed in this role. King. Leader. The righteous chooser who all look to for trust. But there comes a time where one may start to question their own image of who you have presently become. Does it still match the huge tales and shadows of who you once were? Combining stories clash of a powerful story that has taken such a turn of emotion. Can I handle this responsibility? Is it really my choice to decide my own fate? Even though I have never cared for others opinion I have come face to face with my own opinion and TRUTH! Do I like what I see and hear? Can I change it? Can I live up to it? Do I finally understand that my actions speak louder than my words? Proving to myself that my role is indeed hard yet important! Coming to the reality that I have been lucky to fake it and make it this whole time. My people must follow a different King, yet in the same body! The inner struggle with the outer presentation of who I am!!! Countless victories of wars fought throughout this lifetime. Yet the biggest war has yet to come. The greatest enemy just emerging from a distant view. The target has been locked in sight. A strong sense of power has overcome. A familiar chill of who I once was now meets with who I now strive to be. This enemy is great. My allies who accompany me are greater. This all happens in one glance as my eyes stare at my own reflection in the mirror. I am my own enemy. I am my own ally. If the inner me does not match the outer me, nobody will get out of this war alive!

-The Suicide King

AM I A MASTERPEICE IN THE MAKING

Am I a masterpiece in the making? I ask you this because you are the artist that draws my hearts canvas! The strokes of your genius penmanship create my pain and influence my dreams. The brightest of futures scattered into my reality by the thoughts that guide your imagination. It's like I willingly love you with every piece I own just to see you grow more and more proud of the never-ending cycle of our love that you help to create. I am merely a puppet with a mastermind that generates wholehearted love. You make me want to do everything right for the influence of seeing us succeed. True, honest existence just to see you smile. It means the world to me to create this outcome as you stare at it illuminated through the reflection of my eyesight. My whole reason is a willingness to be guided by a blinded storm that clears away all darkness that I have ever grown to know in the end. Sunshine that warms the very deepest parts of a soul and makes everything seem possible to be happy in this moment. It's all too amazing on how you have made me feel ALL this emotion in just the slightest touch from your fingertips to me. It's Heaven on Earth. You are the angel that symphonically balances any insecurities that I may have ever had about love. So, am I now a masterpiece? I feel as I am just a small print of your amazing collection. I am but the smallest line of many things you create with your strong influence on how you touch this canvas of life! Sign your name on my heart and continue to orchestrate the influence of beauty in the way you grace time in the present!

IN MY HUMAN VAULT

Scared shadows hide from me because they know what I intend.

Real life drama, only hoping to wake and realize it's pretended.

As I may sneak up on realities faults, I accept the stored away hopes in my human vault.

Leaving no page blank as I write my next move, hoping to only let adventure guide me into a permanent groove. Can I decide and form this to be the next path? Should I give up and except my days are limited?

Questioning the reasons stored inside and answering with my thoughts. Never spoken out loud just questions that experience has brought. Starring at my shadow, one may never see my scars. Who do I look for, and why are they them? Relationships crumble as I am the only one in the end. No key to get out of my inner human vault, until I met my friend.

She is my locksmith.

4 A MAN WHO CAN'T COMPLAIN

4 a man who can't complain, perfection is always in his sight.
He has no problems in life and can only do things right.
1 foot after the other, a new path is soon to form.
4 a man who can't complain, he cannot avoid the storm.

4 a man who can't complain, he is wet defined by choice.
A small price to pay, as long they can hear his voice.
Soon the storm will pass, and sunshine dries his clothes.
4 a man who can't complain, being fearless surely shows.

4 a man who can't complain, 1 dollar is way too much.
Money is no option when people feel your voice as touch.
Values have no meaning, so it's said in many lies.
4 a man who can't complain, this is looking through my eyes

MY LAST THOUGHT

Hmmm..., how did it get to this point? My final moment in time! Confident that I'm doing the right thing but scared to face what I will never see. How can this be? A single tear slides down my face like the path has been there for years just waiting on the last tear to fall. That tear, the last emotion or feeling that I will ever know. I never thought it would come down to this night. My grip has never been tighter. With one twitch of a muscle that only take 2 pounds of pressure, all that I have become and done for everyone is now obsolete. Now, one tear at a time comes from those who claimed to love me. Well, how did it get to this point if I was loved by so many? Could nobody see the signs? Was I really that good of a faker? Did I lie to myself and others this whole time? So, who is this person? Is it me or just my perception of what I want? I can't tell the difference anymore. My real inner person has met up with my reflection. As I try to tell you my last thought, my grip tightens, breath steady, almost held to remember the silence. Clarity! The smallest pull that took so long to do. Now, thoughts are a thing of my past and yours. My last thought was honestly about you! You are the reason that I have this last thought.

A MOTHER'S PATHWAY

As I walk, on this dirt road...
I think of words that my momma told me.
She said baby boy, you will grow up strong,
But in one short breath it will seem so long.
My mom looked up, and her boy looked down,
Her smile grew as my tears came down.
If I only knew then what I know now,
I'd a walked that road with her somehow.
As your baby boy, I know you made me strong.
Teaching me things right and steered away from wrong.
Momma's love was pure, she gave it all she had. Well life is sometimes hard and then it's sometimes sad.
And as I think of you, I see how angels fly.
Mom I stand here strong, even though I cry!
I wish that you could tell, from the look in my eyes, that your angel wings were always meant for these skies.
I held her hand, her grip was soft, not tight,
Momma slipped away, on that rainy night!
Oh, the memories, as I'm still your baby boy, thoughts I won't forget of your love and joy.
When my spirits down, she raised my spirits high, her boy is now a Man, I say my last goodbye!!!

MOM

It's hard to find the perfect word, when one word has so many definitions. MOM. That alone should send a powerful message. A job like no other. The strongest woman on Earth in my eyes. The one true rock in my world who has never given up on me and always gives words of encouragement. No matter how grown or independent I may have come to be, I will always be looked at as your baby boy. Thank you doesn't cut it. You have literally saved my life more than I could ever repay. Just the words that come from your soul to help me get through tough times and guide me into making the right choices for my future have me in debt to you. You're my teacher. You always paint my picture but let me sign and take credit for it. I'm your secret admirer in life. There is no way I can ever give you the amount of credit you deserve but I can tell you this, thank you! I love you! I'm sorry! I may have made you worry at times but when I wasn't strong enough to hold my head high you were there to lift my chin. You have wiped tears and made me an amazing man! The joy in my heart is overwhelming when I see you with my little boys. The reality of how you treat them is matched with the unknown reality of my childhood. I get to see that love all over again and have a deeper understanding of it! It's a beautiful thing! So here is to you Mom! There will never be just one word to describe all the appreciation and love I have for you! I'm proud to say you are one of my best friends! Loyal! When the world turns MOM upside down, the outcome is WOW! That's because you are amazing!

Love,
Rypoo

MY DAD

My dad! Man, where do I start? A character indeed. A man of many faces. A person that will rise to any occasion. A friend, a father, a family man. So much good in a single spirit. A dime a dozen! My dad.... pure 110% dedicated to any job until it's done. First on the scene and last to leave. He can see both viewpoints of an argument and help both sides understand why each other's reason is right! Neutral but always has your back. The first person I call with a problem or for advice. A straight answer. Genuine, smart, and funny all the time. Sometimes more popular with my friends then I am. Always there when you need a hand or a shoulder. Hard shoes to fill. A good role model for all humans. A retired cop... Excuse me, Officer! A sharpshooter (literally). What a guy! Dad of the year every year! Papa King! My hero! Determined and willing to always go out of the way to help before anyone else. So here is a toast to a man that doesn't drink.... My father, my dad, my pal, my blood.

Thanks man!

MY LITTLE BOY

As the first time I laid eyes on my little boy, a story emerged that would have an ending that I was not sure of. Blinded by the fact that we all live day by day, one could only hope that my little boy would stay. Hopes that he would stay little and always want to play. Hopes that he would look for my advice when he has gone the wrong way. Hopes of just one day he could see things my way. Our hopes are the same, yet very different at times. Independents is rushed just to wish for my little boy to need me more than ever. A full understanding only in a time that is a second too late. What was wanted for so long, is now here,
but certainly, hard to welcome.

LOOKING INTO COOPER'S HEART

Strong. Lovable. Dedicated to giving everything he has for the one shot at getting what he wants in that moment in time. Does not care about the future. He never holds a grudge for anything in the past. Lives now. Loves now. Puts all emotion and all his feelings into everything he touches right then and there. Overcomes challenges by the second. Smarter than what most people give him credit for. Starts most days with a half empty glass because of a condition he did not ask for, but by the end of the day has a glass that over pours with straight love! He endures. He teaches. He lives daily how everyone strives to live, but people surround themselves with lies just to be as carefree and engulfed in love as this little boy. He doesn't know of his fate! I don't really think it will ever take a toll on him anyway! Whoever meets him leaves that day a better person. Has a strong brother. Has a strong father. He has a strong mother. He has his own community that lifts him up and supports him daily! He makes his whole family stronger personally, physically, and mentally. He lives life, loves life, and enjoys life. He wakes up in the middle of the night to laugh and clap. Wakes up in the morning to greet with hugs like it's the first time he has seen you! Loves his puppy! His puppy loves him! We all love him! I love him! I am super thankful! I don't want him normal! I want him just the way he is. If there was a cure, it would be great, but without a cure he changes others' lives and loves living his life despite the negative aspect of what everyone expects. He bounces back. He is a part of my soul I didn't know existed! I'm very lucky to have this experience. This responsibility of life that I get to care for is a test I cannot fail. This is an amazing person I get to share with the world. You hear him before you see him and when you see him you never forget. He is a tattoo of personality on everyone's brain and especially their HEART! Cooper King is my son. Dravet Syndrome is his weakness. But LOVE will always overcome and be his strength!

Daddy loves you Cooper!!!

My Grandmother's Hand

Each wrinkle tells a story of her life and parts of mine I'm proud to say. The hand she used to build her shadow and form the ways of life I see through my eyes. Her hands have brought so much love, through the dinners that our family has shared. Her gentle touch is like an angle's kiss, so comforting in the darkest and most confusing of times in my life. A simple pat on the back from my grandmother's hand can mean so much, more than words could ever explain. My grandmother's hand is so beautiful, surviving through several wars. With her hand she has wiped tears from her own face, to assure that she will live to become a stronger person. Her hands helped clean me up when I was a little boy and straightening my tie as a young man. My grandmother's hands have helped me through a lot. They have signed her name in letters of two different languages to fully define who she is as a person. A person that only I may think I know, but time is the only thing that will hold me back from truly knowing it all. Her hands show me pictures of her past which helps me to understand my heritage. Although a lot may change physically, the same sweet touch will remain. As a comforting, gentle feel from her thumb sliding up and across the top of my hand, lets me know that her warmth and guidance is on my side. Each wrinkle earned in a life that has seen even the darkest second of night. Thinking of her hands may make the darkest times seem bright. The bones may become weak, and the skin may begin to thin. Yet the power, the power of my grandmother's hand grows stronger by the day.

Hands are what make us who we are! My grandmas are great!

GRANDPARENTS 50th WEDDING ANNIVERSARY

It started with a look; their eyes met across a room.
Never knowing that this moment, would turn him into a groom.
They introduced their selves and told stories of their land.
The attraction grew much stronger, now they're hand in hand.
More than hand in hand, they hold each other's hearts.
Wedding bells are sounding, a new family will start.
They did like families do, producing two girls and a boy.
Never even knowing, that it would bring them so much joy.
Time would let the children grow, and memories would form.
Continue guiding as great parents, now grandchildren have been born.
Both have helped and guided me, and have showered me with love.
And, if I didn't know it, I'd guess they were angels from above.
Words cannot express, the way I feel about you two.
I word, seems to work, so I'll simply say, "I Do".

A BEAUTIFUL GIFT

What on Earth have I done to deserve such a beautiful gift? A question that I will never be able to answer unless I can get you to see through the eyes of myself! You couldn't possibly understand how lifelong insecurities and pain all are instantly lifted just from a one second glance from your eyes into mine. A touch that makes me feel like I have healed all sickness in the world for others. Returning faith in so many things that I have lost and never planned on finding again. Not even knowing where to search, yet simply delivered in front of me. Not needing the smallest of steps to hold in my grasp. Why do I get to have you? Because I know that I can give you the same in return! I can be your catch when you have fallen in the deepest abyss. The one to wipe away that tear that would have tipped your bucket of emotions! The guidance to help find the straight pathway of pleasures in life! I feel like I can do this because you balance me and give me the strength to keep you balanced. Equal. Not better, just complimenting you the same way I feel you are there for me. Empathy. Knowing. Wanting to know. Learning. Forgiving. Why? Because we deserve each other! Deserving. Words have no meaning when they are not said yet we speak in silence in full understanding. You feel me look at you. I see you feel me! What happens next? I can't wait to find out!

CUPID'S ASSASSIN

Right in the crosshairs of the sights that are centered hot. Cupid is my assassin who loves to forget me not. Why? Pain that I can heal, forever only I can feel. Lurking in a memory that one can't seal. Cupid takes aim at my heart waiting to see the red spill out of a perfect shot. The feeling over comes my soul as the numbness makes me unaware of the story being told. Cold. Time stops and my feelings for you are returned only to remain on hold. As the arrow pushes deeper into my heart, the feeling is just beginning to spark. Heat. Not from the sun, but the assassins aim. Cupid never misses but his intentions are questioned. Aimed to acknowledge nothing that's true. I mean this because he directed my mercy regarding you! That arrow has never been felt so much. Setting me up for a spill of my cup of hope. Liquid feelings pour through the cracks unable to be soaked up. Wanting to sew my soul back together but it just seems to tear it more apart! Wearing thin, this assassin's arrow is all the way in. Bare to my skin I feel assassin's creed. But no more will I bleed. I take the arrow out. I look away from you! No more blood as I see the world all anew. All because I see a whole new view. The antidote was my realization, that all along the cupid assassin was me!

MY MATCH

Searching for a purpose in life is why we will always keep searching! Creating a purpose in life is why you find happiness! The search is over when the meaning of life turns into the opportunity to make others happy through the experiences you share with others. Not having to think but naturally sharing what comes to mind only to find that you are guiding them in a direction that helps put them on their path to serenity. By spreading the conscious ways of your routine, you meet with someone who comes out of nowhere so unexpectedly and sees your vision. Not only do they see your vision, but they speak your truth. They admire and encourage you to be yourself. This person literally understands the laws of your purpose and nods a paragraph without saying a word. So, you join forces. Undeniable and utterly infatuated with sharing a common idea of how to spend the rest of each other's days in a common agreement. The purpose, to see beauty in making each other happier than the day before. A team. One heartbeat. Yours for her heart and hers for yours. Checkpoints are significantly scattered across the world only for us to connect these dots of the adventure we share while we both hold the pen together. An absolute amazing journey filled with all emotions. Only to know that we will always be there in times to look in each other's eyes and know that we have this journey to look forward to together. Fun. Love. The rush of letting each other control life at any given moment. Knowing and trusting that we will not only be ok but also have an amazing time together with whoever takes the wheel. An amazing comfort. A striving effort that most fake but we achieve with ease. I'm so excited every day and more so for knowing I will be the same in 10 years from now! I have finally met my match! But before our game of life begins, we call it a draw, only to never stick around to see who has won. Before they announce to the audience, we have already left on this playground called Earth to see what else we can share together. To us, "together" is a win! No matter how big or how small the roof is above, no matter how full or small the ration on the plate, I am happy with your smile and your hand in mine! With that alone I can say the world is now OURS to play with.

My Vow

The first time I laid eyes on you in a picture it took my breath away. The moment I saw you in real life, my breath was taken away because you looked even better in front of me. Today I look at you and my breath is still taken away because the thought of sharing the rest of our time together has set in. I'm lucky. I only wish you could see yourself through my eyes. I admire you. You have made me a better person. A better man. I hope I can be the best husband and friend to you. I will set an example as best I can to show our boys how to treat the one, they love. I will defend you, love you, laugh and cry with you. I'm excited to paint this beautiful masterpiece of "Our Life" with both of our hands holding the brush together. In this, our faults will stay for us to learn from. Our life will be painted from our adventures we take together. Our rings represent our signature of our masterpiece to seal our claim to this amazing life we are about to create and share together.

This path was created long before we had met.

TAKE A WALK WITH ME BABY IN THE GA RED CLAY

Take a walk with me baby in the GA red clay!
Hand in my hand, tell me how you wanna play.
Long hard kisses, on a bud light night.
Twirl you around, underneath the moonlight.
Stepping in the shadows, but you are a bright light,
if loving you is wrong, girl you know I ain't right.
Get a little muddy, but we're having lots of fun,
loving you forever underneath the Georgia sun.

Came into the picture, my eyes zeroed in on you!
Chills kicked in as I had a drink or 2.
Knew it right then, I wanted you to be mine.
Chase me with tequila, you could be my little lime.
Dance with me baby, on this Georgia red clay.
Barefooted momma, girl you know I'm here to stay.

Ask me no more questions and tell me no more lies.
Wrap around me baby, with those American thighs.
Tell me all your secrets and whisper to me in my ear.
Let me have your heart and I'll take away your fear.

Put your hand in mine, as we're riding on the clay.
Sitting in the middle right next to me today.
Girl I'll tell you once, but I never tell you twice
Keep you flowing like a river as we shaking up some dice
Shaking on the dice ready steady let'em go.
Push the pedal down and rev me up, girl we never go slow.

Call it dirty dancing on this GA red clay.

THOUGHTS FROM A KING

Cause I'm all about you mamma and you know I am here to stay.
When it comes to those lips, wouldn't have it no other way.
When it comes to those hips, man you know she don't play.
Dance with me mamma, girl you shake it on this clay.
Walking with my Georgia peach, on a hot summer day.

Thoughts of you on this Earth

Seems to me, the longest moment in time is that when you start to walk away, only to be overcome by joy when our eyes meet again. The anticipation of a short night's sleep, just to awaken of the thought of you, my love. The longing last goodbye under a moon so bright is countered by a warm hello of your voice of a yawning sunrise. Sensational feeling of your lips when they meet mine when you arrive in my arms. A feeling I can't explain when I know we think the same thoughts of appreciation for each other. Perfection like I have never imagined. You just want my attention, my love, and my affection. I have never been wanted and have never wanted to give all these things to someone as much as I intended to give to you. A tear from your eye will always be welcomed in a joyous occasion and will always be wiped away in concerns of any negative emotion I sense from you. You are the ocean that covers my heart, and the tide of your love controls the pull of my direction that keeps bringing me back for more of your love. Engulfed and completely lost in the abyss of the future pathway of our story. Exciting and comfortable. Easily anticipating whatever happens next because I know your hand will be in mine and your eyes will be set on mine. Our hearts will beat in rhythm, and I can honestly say I am completely in love with the most beautiful woman on this crazy Earth.

To A Man I've Never Met.

My respect for you is great. I see her loyalty for you, and it will never go away. I want to share my thoughts with you although I'll never see your face. I see the bar that you have set for her. My plan is not to take your place. I gladly listen to all her stories of the good times and the bad. To guide her and your little boy in times that are happy and even sad. I hope you understand this sir, my intentions are strictly for the best. Your soul will live through us all, and your memories may peacefully rest. As time may carry on through life, I wish you to watch over us. Guide us in the righteous path as I will try to provide a positive, safe and understanding environment for the ones you cherished most. Life is definitely not fair; I can tell she feels the same. Even though we have not met, we share Kimberly the same. She is amazing to me, and I know she was to you. I just want your blessing sir; this is my request to you. I feel it is only right to get approval from the two most important people in her life. Your little boy may read this letter one day, right now it's for your wife. I'll join her on the days that remind her of you the most! Her hand may be in mine now sir, but you will always be in our toasts! So here I write this letter sir, to a man I've never met! So, when the time does come to meet... a handshake is what I'll get! Trust in me, and watch over us, as I plan to give this my all!

You

I could draw your face in my mind even if I had no way to see like the blind. I know the feeling of your touch as if you were lying your sole on my chest. Never could I rest, if I knew that I could prevent even the slightest bit of harm or uneasiness to you. It's you. That word alone sends a shiver throughout my body. So much hate, so much love. So overwhelming due to the absolute infatuation that I have for you. My feelings for you are stronger than the moment that some get knowing to cherish a last goodbye. Why do I cry? It is because my vision is everything to make you fully believe in me of our present relationship. I could never imagine life without you. Even through times where I can't stand to be around you. It's all in vain. Just because you don't follow my expectations, doesn't mean I should act upon it. This is the reason I fell so hard for you in the first place. You! No other could amount or share exactly what we have made. You! The reason for my hate, love, fear, insecurities, and most of all for my will to be a better person. Each day trying to make you fall deeper in love with me. But does love have a pinnacle? Is it an endless account that will always have room for the misery of such a guilty pleasure? Honest love! The goal of every human's existence. You can make or break me, a power that I'm sure you'll never know the true strength of. I could only hope that one day you, could see me, the same way that I see you.

My love,

you!

Frustrations I have,
I cannot be controlled now.
Am I the bad guy?

A big chance I took,
Our eyes met, I'm on one knee,
She cries, says, "I do".

Helping students learn,
Setting examples for them,
Guide them to success.

Dear Mr. King, Thanks!
I learned through your example.
Cheers, to our success!

Young driver driving
Loud screech, bang, crash. Now silent!
The text was not sent.

My best friend is great
Her hair has always been gray,
My Schnauzer, Vera.

Old couple's last kiss,
It took 60 years to make.
A sad but earned kiss.

Today's playground rules
Use your imagination
That's the only rule.

A treat on a stick
Fresh batter, dipped down to cook.
Ketchup meet corndog.

Born from cookie dough
Now give me a glass of milk
A delicious treat.

I like chicken stew.
What is chicken stew you ask?
Secret recipe.

I give when I can.
Never know what good it does,
More than your eyes' see.

www.ingramcontent.com/pod-product-compliance
Ingram Content Group UK Ltd.
Pitfield, Milton Keynes, MK11 3LW, UK
UKHW051207260726
13967UKWH00011B/3155

9 781638 371724